The Days of Golf

Playing the Greatest Game in Dallas

By

Sandy McDonough

"Golf is a wonderful walk in nature often spoiled by a little white ball." Unknown

"As you walk down the fairway of life you must smell the roses along the way because you just get one round." Ben Hogan

"Golf and Sex are the only things you can enjoy without being good at them". Jimmy Demaret

"The only time God doesn't answer my prayers is when I am on the golf course." The Reverend Billy Graham

The Days of Golf

Playing the Greatest Game in Dallas

ISBN # 978-0-615-95931-3

This book is dedicated to the memory of my father, Sam McDonough, a fine golfer to be sure, but more importantly, a kind and gracious southern gentleman, loving father and God's faithful servant.

The Course

Acknowledgements

I am grateful to many for providing the fond memories that made this endeavor possible. Special thanks to Marilyn Munger for locating the treasure trove of family photographs and sharing her recollections. Thanks also to John Colwick and Tom Newsome for their input and remembrances. I am very appreciative to the following authors for their research in publishing their pictorial histories of Country Clubs:
A History of Northwood by Art Stricklin
Brook Hollow Golf Club by Rhonda Glenn
DCC 1896-Centennial-1996 by Diane Galloway with Gifford Touchstone and Ed Doran
A Dallas Classic Lakewood Country Club by Curt Sampson

And thanks to my golfing pals over the years who are far too numerous to mention. And thanks to my family, especially my father and mother, who taught me the greatest game.

Fore

A large part of my early years in Dallas were spent at country clubs playing golf, tennis, swimming, or just simply hanging out. Those were the carefree fun-filled days that upon reflection continue to fuel fond memories today. I spent virtually every day on the golf course, tennis courts, or in the swimming pool. On other occasions our family would go to the club to participate in special activities like the annual Easter egg hunts, the 4th of July fireworks show, birthday parties, banquets and dances. While my parents and their close circle of friends belonged to Northwood, many other friends were members of the Brook Hollow Golf Club or the Dallas Country Club. So it was no problem getting on a course. With golf being our #1 main common interest, the "golf casuals" emerged which aptly described a group of guys who loved to play the game by day and party by night. The following pages recall some of the fond reflections. Those were truly the good ol' days when golf was king!

Northwood

One summer day in 1946, several friends were playing tennis at Brook Hollow Golf Club. Afterwards, they discussed the idea of creating a new country club to the north of a burgeoning Dallas. At the time some of the older clubs such as the Dallas Country Club and Brook Hollow Golf Club had waiting lists and the friends envisioned a new club. Northwood Club was born that day by doubles partners Estil Heyser, Billy Moore, Hugh Prather, and John Pace. Hick Majors, a Dallas realtor, was selected to find a suitable location for a new club. One of the sites being considered was a 160-acre ranch spread far north of Dallas on Alpha Road between Preston Rd. and Hillcrest Ave that belonged to oilmen Buddy Fogelson and Clint Murchison. Fogelson agreed to sell his home and his surrounding property for the sum of $165,000 with $65,000 down and a $100,000 loan for the balance of the note. Fogelson, after a divorce, had married movie star Greer Garson. Their sprawling one story ranch house that was built in 1938 became the clubhouse. Later that summer several organizational meetings were held and initial memberships were offered. Dad and 99 others paid $100 each as charter members of the new club.

Construction began in earnest on the golf course, tennis courts and pool. When more money was needed to complete the facilities, slot machines were brought in to raise additional capital. Lifetime memberships were offered and Roy Munger and Jack Flippen ponied up $5000 each for these memberships to help defray the rising costs. Billy Moore was elected the first president. Jack Munger, a noted amateur golfer, recommended William Diddle of Indianapolis be the golf course architect along with Perry Maxwell. Ralph Plummer would be the supervisor overseeing the golf course. The new 18-hole course officially opened on April 17, 1948, with Jack Munger fittingly hitting the first ball. My mother Virginia "Ginny" McDonough was selected to be the first woman to tee off on the new course from the woman's tees.

I was six years old at the time the golf course opened and by now was very familiar with the new club and its amenities. The old horse stables were there for a while during the early beginnings and I remember riding horses, taking swimming lessons and playing tennis. The swimming pool was quite large with a small wading baby pool off to the side. The men and women's locker rooms flanked each side of the deep end. And there was a hamburger, hot dog and refreshment stand. We also dined inside the new club where cheeseburgers and Early's famous frozen cherry oranges were my favorites. My parents would drive my sister Ginger, brother Mike and me in the Olds to the club, which was a distance of about 12 miles from our home. Our usual route took us north on Preston Road, which was back then a two-lane country road that ran through a few sparse neighborhoods, a smattering of farms and undeveloped land. A right turn on Alpha Road led to the new club. If we drove up north on Hillcrest Ave we took a left turn onto Alpha and crossed over White Rock Creek to the club.

At times, while driving to the club, we would stop and pick up caddies along the road who were thumbing for a ride. The caddies gathered together outside the golf shop off the 9th hole green in what was known as the "caddie pen." During the early years there were no golf carts so the caddies would often carry two bags for $5.00 each. Some earned money by being "spotters" staying ahead of the golfers to locate their balls. My spotter was named "Money" and he made sure I never had a bad lie. I remember some of their unique names: Gump, the caddie master, Sammy, the bag master, Rock, Raydale, and Gizmo.   Inside the men's locker room was Gabriel Thomas, aka "Sea Level" as he was affectionately known because of his diminutive stature. The first pro was Harry Todd whose wife and my mother formed the first ladies golf league at Northwood. James and Early were bartenders; and one of the erstwhile waitresses was Eleanor who served the dining patrons for decades. The first manager was "Blackie" and then Royce Cheney.   Floyd Hightower was the swimming instructor who taught me how to swim across the pool without drowning.

During the week there were no restrictions on the number of golfers who could play together. Thus was formed the gangsome. The number of golfers in the gangsome might range from five to ten or even more depending on who showed up; all loved to play the game and gamble. The gambling was often complex and frequently needed an accountant with a CPA to sort out all the scores, the side bets, etc. The final figuring was usually done in the 19th hole after a few beverages.   There were bets and side bets on the front nine, back nine and on the 18.   There were automatic 2 down presses, plus bonuses paid for sandies, birdies, eagles, closest to the hole on par 3's and so on. Back then when someone or a team won $50 that was a big deal. At times I was invited to play with the gangsome.   One day I shot the lowest score of 74 with 4 birdies and won over $50.   Some of the gangsome regulars back in those days were my father, Bob Quinlan, Al Couchman, Jim Wade, Mo Messenger, Jack Munger, Lewis Lyne, Brud Smith, Art Hammer, Bill Newsome, Les Stemmons, Grady Prim, W. L. Todd, Collett Munger, J.B. Hudnall, Leslie Schultz, Gene Emery and others.

I truly enjoyed playing golf with dad and mom who taught me the game at an early age.   Dad was an exceptionally fine golfer with a smooth graceful swing and he was especially deadly on the greens with his old wood shaft putter. He normally carried a 3 or 4 handicap and had 4 aces on the par 3 5th hole.   He won the Northwood Club

Championship in 1950 defeating his good friend Jack Munger who had won the tournament the previous two years. One highlight came later when his good friend and golfing buddy Lew Lyne invited him to play at Augusta National the home of the Masters. He and Lew were flown to Augusta on Jack Stephens's private jet. Once there, Dad had dinner with Cliff Roberts, the "King of Augusta National," who had the final say so on who got to play. Dad was "approved" and had wonderful memories of his trip. Most of all, Dad was a true southern gentleman and I cannot ever remember him getting mad or tossing a club.

Calcutta Pool. Dad 2nd from left after winning Northwood Club Championship   That's me in the striped shirt.

Around the time of the formation of Northwood, my mother (2nd from left 1st row) and three of her lady friends-Caroline Lyne, Rene Lubben, and Sunny Clemens formed the "Thirsty Thursday" Club at our home on Edmondson. The club became the longest running gin rummy game in Dallas.   The ladies played cards every Thursday afternoon for over 60 years!   Mom and her group, which expanded to over 20 during the ensuing years, included Caroline Lyne, Jane and Marion Munger, Muggye Chilton, Rene Lubben, Jean Hammer, Sunny Clemens, Jerry Smith, Ruth Rowe, Tootie Bush, Betty Hudnall, Lillian Grady, Marty Reid, Mary Louise Lingo, Madeline Wade, Fran Messenger and others. The ladies would often gather in the card room at Northwood or The Dallas Country Club or someone's home for an afternoon of gin rummy or bridge. The Thirsty Thursday group remained intact until well into the 21st century when it faded away as age took its toll.

"El Mungo"

Jack R. Munger was considered to be one of the best amateur golfers in the country and certainly one of golf's more unique personalities. Affectionately known as "El Mungo" or "The Great Mungo" to his pals, he participated in various tournaments from coast to coast and overseas for over 30 years. He won numerous national and state amateur titles starting in the early 1930's. He began playing golf at the age of 11 and never stopped until his death at 59. At the age of 17 in 1932 he was the 3rd low amateur in the USGA Open. He reached the semi-finals of the USGA Amateur in 1933 and the quarterfinals in 1935. He won several major amateur tittles including the Eastern Interscholastic Golf Championship in 1933, the Southern Amateur in 1936 in Memphis, and the Bobby Jones Four Ball at the Southern Amateur in 1951.

Jack played in the first Masters, 5th from right top row, in 1934. He was in outstanding company with Walter Hagen, Bobby Jones, Gene Sarazen, Craig Wood, and Horton Smith. He played the Masters the next year where Gene Sarazen hit the "shot heard around the world"- a four wood for a double eagle 2 on the 15th hole that got him into a playoff that he won the next day. Munger said Bobby Jones was the best all around player he had seen, although Byron Nelson was the greatest shot maker. Jack watched Jones win 2 of his grand slam tournaments in 1930. Munger finished 28th in the 1936 U.S Open. He won the Colorado State Amateur Championship in 1948. In a member-guest tournament at Cherry Hills in Denver in 1953, Jack fired a course record 63 that was witnessed by President Dwight D Eisenhower who was vacationing there.

1953 photo at the Broadmoor

Mungo cut a striking figure on the links. I saw him on television on the 18th green in the Bing Crosby Invitational at Pebble Beach. He was wearing colorful Scottish knickers, a tam o'shanter, and chomping on his proverbial long big cigar. When he holed his putt, he broke into an Irish jig. He and his team were runners-up at the Crosby Invitational in 1959. The flamboyant professional Walter Hagen had nothing on him. Mungo was quite the bon vivant: fun loving, joking, and frequently boisterous as was

Hagen.   Jack and his amateur partner Bobby Riegel played Hagen and Dick Metz in a charity match at the Dallas Country Club in 1941.   Hagen was the president of the Ryder Cup that year and, as Munger tells it, Hagen was up all-night and late to the first tee.   Jack and Riegel won the match on the last hole.

Jack had some rather unique expressions such as "bullburgers and banana pie" and "My God, you look like a busted bale of hay."   On the course one could hear him several holes away especially if he or his partner hit a good shot.   In Dallas, he and his wife Jane Hopkins Munger belonged to the "big three" country clubs, Brook Hollow, Dallas and Northwood.   His extended family was instrumental in the founding and development of Lakewood Country Club, Dallas Country Club, Brook Hollow Golf Club, and Northwood Club.   The couple was known around North Texas as "Mr. and Mrs. Golf".

Jack was President of the Trans- Mississippi Golf Association in 1958, 1959, and 1960 and a director of the Western Golf Association.   He and Jane filled their trophy cases with local country club championships: Jack won club championships at Dallas Country Club in 1939 and 1940, Brook Hollow in 1935, 1939, 1941 and 1948, and Northwood in 1948, 1949, and 1951.   Jane was a 4-time ladies champion at Northwood, a 5-time champion at Dallas Country Club and a 9-time champion at Brook Hollow.   My Dad interrupted Jack's string of victories at Northwood by defeating his friend for the club championship in 1950.   Jack held the course record at Northwood with a 64 that was tied by professionals Raymond Gafford, Dudley Wysong, Billy Maxwell, Justin

Leonard and the current professional Bob Elliott. Some of the better Dallas amateur golfers of that era were Don Schumaker, Harry Todd, Bobby Riegel, Reynolds Smith, Dennis Lavender, Gus Moreland, David "Spec" Goldman, Jack Tinnin, Charlie Dexter, Billy Bob Coffee, Edwin Hopkins, Herb Durham and O'Hara Watts.

The stories about "El Mungo" are legendary. One often repeated is that during World War II, while serving overseas in the Army, he was invited to play golf with the King of Egypt and afterwards he dined in the royal palace in Cairo with the Royal Family. During his service in the war he played many rounds with generals on European golf courses. He also won several tournaments during his service including one in Casablanca.

Munger Place and Lakewood Country Club

The Munger families, early pioneers in Dallas, developed Munger Place in the Lakewood area of east Dallas. Jack's father Roy Munger was an excellent golfer and an early member of the Dallas Country Club and Brook Hollow. Roy won the City Championship and played in the National Amateur several times. He was the President of Brook Hollow in 1933, 1934, and 1935 and served as President of the Dallas Country Club. Jack's grandfather, Stephen (S.I.) Munger, his brother Robert, and Robert's oldest son Collett, were instrumental in developing Lakewood and East Dallas. Not long after the State of Texas became a Republic, Robert's family lived near Mexia and had a thriving cotton gin business. Over the years he improved the cotton gin and built a large manufacturing business that was the source of the family's wealth. The Mungers migrated north to Dallas, sold the business and began acquiring acreage east of the city that became Munger Place in 1905, the first planned community in Dallas. This was the earliest deed restricted neighborhood in Texas with homes to be two stories, prairie-style designed, situated on large tree lined lots with paved streets, sewers, gas mains, electric street lights and sidewalks. Building costs ranged from $2,000 to $10,000 and homes were sold to the "elite." During the depression the homes and the neighborhood deteriorated. A revival began in the 1970s as Dallas real estate developers began to buy, restore and rebuild the dilapidated homes. In 1980 the City of Dallas designated Munger Place as a historical district.

Munger Place Homes

During the time that Lakewood was being developed, the newly created town of Highland Park under the leadership of Hugh Prather and Edgar Flippen was attempting to lure the first country club in Texas, the Dallas Country Club, to move from their Oak Lawn location to be the focal point of their new town. Perhaps taking a cue, Collett Munger and his Uncle Stephen formed the Dallas Development Company to purchase property in and around Munger Place for a country club. Some 274 acres were accumulated of which 188 acres were sold in August 1912 to the new development company. The total cost of the property was $27,000 with only $5,400 down – quite a deal! On October 31, 1912, the State of Texas issued a charter certifying Lakewood Country Club.

LAKEWOOD COUNTRY CLUB, DALLAS.

Ed Dudley
Bob Hope
E.L Smith
Jack Munger
Bob Schemrlane

After Jack
returned from the war, he and Jane welcomed many
returning soldiers in their home. His daughter Marilyn
tells the story that Jane had hired a secretary Ann without
telling Jack. One day after Jack emerged from the bedroom
there was Ann – "Yikes who are you!" She replied, "Why,
I am your new secretary!" Despite his bluster and
flamboyancy, Mungo was quite generous donating much of
his time and money to charities to help those who were less
fortunate. He got me a job one summer at Winter Dobson,
the local Munsingwear distribution store he owned on
Greenville Avenue that carried the popular Lacoste golf
shirts. He also was a partner in the Village Man's Shop.

Sometime in the late 40s, Jack, Jane and their daughter
Marilyn moved to his father Roy's estate near the
intersection of Preston Road and Beverly Drive. The new
location was convenient since it was within a wedge shot to
the DCC. A few years later, during the remodeling of their
home on Seneca, they lived upstairs in one of the large 3rd
floor bedrooms at the Dallas Country Club. The Mungers
entertained often, and, as their daughter Marilyn recalls,

By now they had hired George who maintained their home, did the cooking, bartended and shopped. George remained with the family for fifty- five years!   His ubiquitous presence with the family was so well known by everyone that he would become known as George Munger. George was a very creative cook, who often made the Thirsty Thursday club ladies his special hors d'oeuvres. Everyone's favorite was his famous "cheesies." When the Mungers lived on Seneca I remember someone yelled, "send the drinks up with the dumb waiter!" Not knowing that a dumb waiter was a lift that brought drinks up from the kitchen, I thought that was a rude thing to say to George!   I remember well that summer day when our families were swimming in their pool and my young brother Mike jumped into the deep end and went under. Fortunately, I saw him and dove in to pull him out.   The Mungers had one of the first televisions and Ginger, Mike and I loved going to Seneca to watch those great old black and white TV shows.

The Broadmoor

During the 50s several Dallas families often took summer vacations in Colorado Springs. Our family often stayed at the Broadmoor or the Garden of the Gods and played great golf courses. Jane Munger's mother owned a home near the Broadmoor and, after a day of golf, it often served as the evening scene for cocktail parties. The Broadmoor hosted the popular "If you must strain your milk" golf tournament where movie stars, singers, corporate heads and great amateur golfers gathered from all over the country such as Gordon MacRae, Bob Goldwater, Dinah Shore, Phil Harris, Michael T Hallibouty, Bob Hope and others.

Broadmoor "strain your milk" golfers and partygoers.   1967

One day I played golf with Jack at the Boadmoor. On this trip he brought along his personal caddy "Jinx" from the Dallas Country Club.   After a few holes, Jack asked Jinx to unzip the ball pocket and hand him the liquid contents contained therein.   The vodka certainly seemed to have no adverse affect on his game as he went on to shoot a 68.

Ginny Lang, Paula Petrie, Dinah Shore, Jane   1966 Broadmoor

The longest drive I ever had was on a high altitude course in Evergreen, Colorado. It was on a 520-yard par 5 with a strong wind behind me. I took a big swing and struck the ball dead solid perfect on the screws and watched it soar over a hill coming to rest about 100 yards from the green.

Several Dallas families, including ours, rented vacation homes during the summer in Cuernavaca. Golf was on the agenda just about every day. We played courses in San Miguel, Acapulco, Taxco, and Mexico City. In Cuernavaca, Dad and I played with Jack at the local Club de Golf. One day Jack made a hole in one there and upon returning to the 19th hole he ordered drinks for everyone at the club. On another day the three of us played 18 at the Club de Golf in Mexico City with the home pro Roberto de Vicenzo.

Back home we played one day at Shady Oaks in Ft. Worth as a guest of Marvin Leonard who was the founder of Colonial and the CEO of Leonard Department Stores in Ft. Worth. Afterwards, I got to meet Ben Hogan who considered it his home course. To this day I cherish the many rounds of golf that I played with my parents and Jack and Jane Munger who taught me much about the game of golf.

Mom and Dad at La Costa

Mom at Northwood Club Championship

The 1952 US Open

It was considered to be at best a pipe dream by one man that the U.S. Open would come to Northwood Country Club. The members scoffed at the idea, especially since the course was virtually so new in its infant stage. Also, as everyone knows, the summers in Texas were brutal with over 100 degree temperatures a sure bet. But that was the dream of Jack Munger whose solo quest was to bring golf's most prestigious tournament to Northwood. Only two previous Opens had ever been played west of the Mississippi. Despite the skeptics, Munger set out for Far Hills, New Jersey, in the spring of 1950 to meet with the USGA board and its president Joseph Dey to pitch the new club as a contender. Several members of the USGA board knew Munger and his stellar amateur golf record.

A few months later a letter arrived from the USGA informing Northwood that it was indeed being considered as a possible site for the 1952 tournament. However, there were some conditions that needed to be addressed. One of those conditions would be the removal of the large oak tree standing in the fairway on number 6. The hole had been playing as a par 5 for the members, but the USGA wanted to make it a par 4 for the tournament. Some of the members objected to its removal, which could jeopardize getting the tournament. One morning the tree was found mysteriously lying across the fairway with evidence that it had been sawed down overnight. According to legend, it was strongly rumored that Jack Munger chopped the offending tree down during the night thus removing the obstruction and the condition imposed by the USGA and clearing the way for the tournament to proceed. A letter of final acceptance soon arrived confirming that Northwood would indeed be the site of the US Open. Game on!

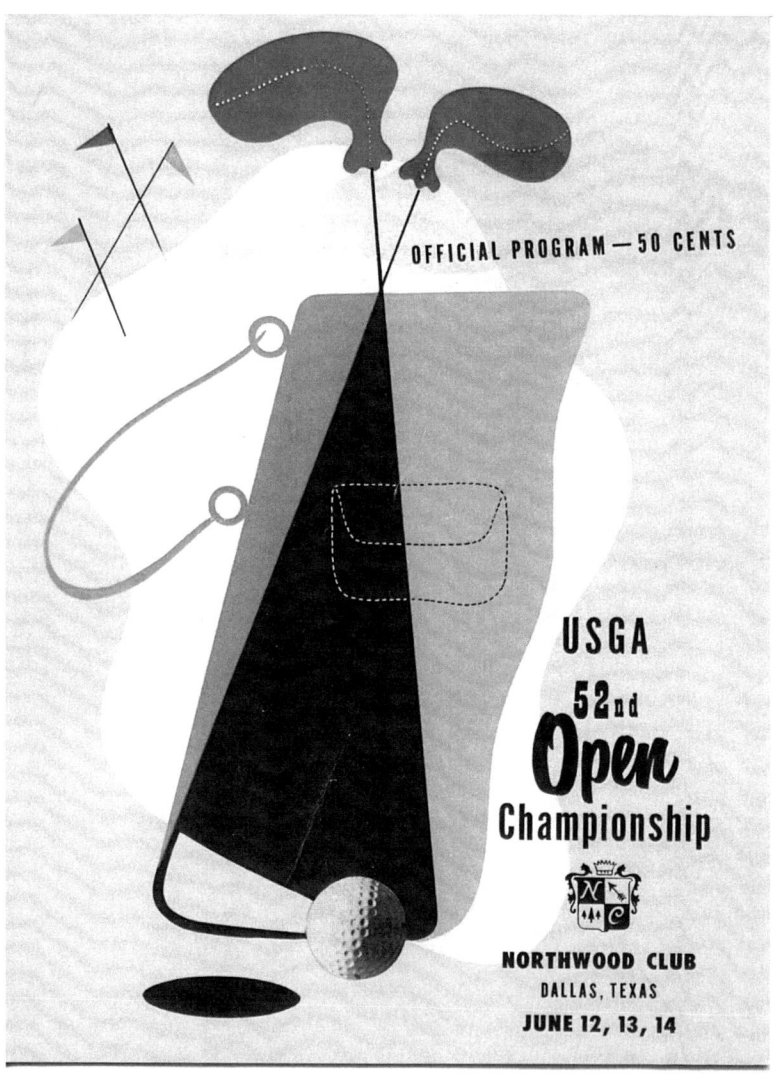

The planning began in earnest right away. Committees were established: My dad was in charge of parking my mother was be in charge of ticket sales. Jack, naturally, was in charge of the golf course.

The Open was held on June 12th, 13th, and 14th 1952. Ben Hogan had come back and was at the top of his game

after suffering some serious injuries from a terrible automobile accident in 1949 that badly injured his legs. After a long rehabilitation process he was the favorite. He had won the US Open in 1948, 1950, and 1951. In the weeks preceding the tournament, Hogan drove over from his home in Ft. Worth to Northwood to hit hundreds of practice balls at the range. I would watch him with awe as he hit long irons with uncanny accuracy dropping the shots within a few feet of a distant caddy. "Bantam Ben" as he was called was all business and had no time for small talk. My mother scored for him during the tournament and she shared this story with me: "On the first tee Mr. Hogan came over to me, and, after politely introducing himself, he said, 'I must have silence to concentrate so please do not talk to me during the round." Another story is that an amateur golfer, after playing with Hogan, was asked if he (Hogan) ever said anything during the round. Yes, he replied, he said, "You're away!"

My Dad tells the story of Sam Snead who fired a low score in a practice round the first time he saw the course. After the round Snead remarked what a "great golf course" complimenting those who had worked so hard to get it in shape. But after the tournament

his tone was decidedly different. Tying for 9th some 12 shots behind the winner Julius Boros, he compared the course to a "cow pasture". During the tournament I would usually wait for the golfers along the 9th green. One day, the South African golfer Bobby Locke came over and gave me his autograph. A photo of this appeared the next day in the Dallas Times Herald.

Hogan finished 3rd, 5 shots behind the winner Julius Borus, and Porky Oliver finished 2nd,4 shots back. Hogan was in contention for another open title until the long par 4 6th hole, when, during the final round, he hit what appeared to be a great second shot. The ball landed hard on the sun-baked green and bounded into Alpha Rd costing him a 2-stroke penalty. Boros, known as a great scrambler, was able to get it up and down a dozen times on the final 18. For his first place finish Boros won $4000, Oliver $2500, and Hogan $1000. Our Northwood home pro, Raymond Gafford, tied for 28th.

12,711 tickets were sold for the tournament and Northwood netted $5,918 after all expenses.

Julius Boros is presented the Championship Trophy

On June 14th 2012, Northwood commemorated the 1952 US Open with a 60-year celebratory dinner that was filmed by ESPN. That evening four golfers who played in the tournament shared their personal reminiscences. Dan Jenkins and Chuck Cooperstein were the MCs and Herb Durham, Dow Finsterwald, Don January and Bill Trombley were the golfers.

Above: With Herb Durham and Brooks Patrick.

Rt.: With Don January

I actually played much more tennis than golf during those early years at Northwood. At first there were only 3 green rubico courts before a couple of hard surface courts were built. Our first pro was Pro Jones who shortly left to be the head pro at the DCC. "Pro" was also the first pro at Brook Hollow and ran a tennis shop in the Highland Park Village. Some of the players I hit with back then were Bruce "Smokey" Swenson, Harvey Davis, Mike Amis and Fred Turner. but mostly the backboard.

There were some very good players at Northwood. The best doubles combos on the courts were the Swensons and the Pensons. Nancy Swenson and her husband Bruce, and Nancy Penson and her husband Jack, played tennis virtually daily. The two Nancys teamed up to win many state tournaments and were nationally ranked. Nancy Swenson was also an accomplished golfer who won both the golf and tennis championship at the DCC in the same year.

Wayne Sabin was hired as the pro during the 50's and was followed by Armando Vieira. I was selected to be a ball boy for the Jack Kramer Tennis Tour that came to Moody Coliseum for which I received an autographed tennis racquet.

The Scanlon families were also excellent players. Bill Scanlon was one of the best players in the world for a while. He reached the finals of Wimbledon by beating John McEnroe in the semi-finals. I was the tennis captain at Highland Park Jr. High and continued playing on the high school team until my junior year when I switched over to the golf team.

During the long hot summer days several of us could be found on the links at Northwood. Charles Martin, Tommy Newsome, Howard Johnsen, John Colwick, Frank Malone, Jimmy Hudnall, and Bob Ransdell were usually there looking for a game. When I was about 9 or 10, I met John Colwick, a natural golfer who shot rounds in the low 80's. Soon thereafter he was shooting par. He became my golfing pal during those days and we played countless rounds together. It was not uncommon for us to play 27 or more holes from morning until darkness forced us off the course.

John was a long hitter who often drove the par 4 first hole. One day at the par 3 12th hole at Northwood, he made a memorable par that will go down as the best par I have ever seen. After hitting his tee shot into the lake, John re-teed another ball hitting it straight into the hole without a bounce!

We played in a few head to head matches in local tournaments. One summer during the Dallas Times Herald Jr. Golf Championship we both made it to the semi -finals. We were playing at Stevens Park and it was one of the rare times that I bested John. The next day I lost in the finals to Kenny Goldman. John won the Northwood Club Championship in 1962 beating W. L. Todd in the finals. He shoots his age these days.

Highland Park Golf Team Threesome
Pictured above are Coach Casey, John Colwick, Kenny Goldman and me.   Other HP golfers not pictured are Tommy Abbott, Bobby Abbott, Mack Strother, Barry Blanton, David Grafe, Frank Malone, Tracy Taylor, Jeff Voss, Danny Cheetum and Steve Summers.

In 1958, John's father, Mr. O. J. Colwick, invited us to Tulsa Oklahoma to see the US Open Championship at Southern Hills Country Club.   We mostly followed Gary Player who was playing in his first United States Open and was dressed in all black reportedly to keep in the 100+ degree heat. "Terrible" Tommy Bolt won the tournament and Player finished second. Mr. Colwick had made prior arrangements for us to play the course the following

Monday. We were on the front nine when I unfortunately shanked a wedge with the ball striking Mr. Colwick on the cheek. By the time we got to the clubhouse a large knot had developed that required medical attention. While he was kept in Tulsa overnight, John and I took a cab to the airport to fly home. In the cab with us was Julius Borus. Thankfully, Mr. Colwick recovered soon enough.

When I went off to college my golf game suffered a bit as did my grades for what some would say were the years of a misspent youth.   I spent my freshman year at the University of Texas mostly playing the guitar, bowling, playing cards, drinking beer and at times attending class. It was there I met Joe Don Looney but that is quite another story. After my freshman year I was back in Dallas in summer school at SMU. After class it was off to the links. Those were the days of the golf casuals. The routine consisted of morning school, afternoon golf and nocturnal partying. Some would refer to us correctly as "golf bums."

After graduating from Baylor, I entered the Marine Corps, spending 6 months in Southern California, two months of boot camp in San Diego and then off to Camp Pendleton for more training. One Saturday I decided to hitch hike to the Camp Pendleton Golf Course to play golf. That would prove to be a fortuitous decision. I rented some clubs and started out playing solo. Midway through the front nine I invited a twosome coming up from behind me in a cart to hit up. It turned out to be the base Commander and his wife. Major General Bruno Hochmuth was one of the most decorated Marines in history and had served his country with distinction in wars abroad and held many posts stateside. After finishing the round the General asked me, "Private, would you like to be on my Marine Corps Golf Team!" "Yes Sir!" I quickly responded. He then gave me a lift in his jeep back to my barracks at San Onofre and told our CO that a Major would be coming by in the morning to take Private McDonough to play golf. Some of the officers were astonished when the major indeed picked me up and we drove off to play courses in Southern California! Nice duty! Major General Hochmuth was tragically killed in Vietnam on November 14, 1967, when his helicopter crashed near Hue.

It was important to keep your shots in the fairway when playing southern California courses because there was no telling what you might find in the rough. I sliced one way off the fairway one day into some sand and brush. Coiled around the ball was a large rattlesnake that made his presence known. I immediately declared it an unplayable lie while scampering back to the fairway.

On another occasion I played the Rancho Santa Fe Country Club course with Glen Miller, a friend of Jack and Jane Munger, who, with his lovely wife Lilo and son lived in La Jolla. Going from Marine Corps military training to playing golf in Southern California was wonderful! When the going gets tough then the tough head to the links! Life was great!

But when my six-month tour of duty was up, I opted to go home to be with my folks, my friends, and, of course, the golf casuals.

That's me with the afro and my partner Dr. Henderson rt.
Great Southwest Golf Club in Arlington, Texas.

For many years there was an informal and fun golf
circuit known as the "Beer and Bar-B-Q" circuit or the
"East Texas Tour". The tournaments were held in many
small Texas towns such as Kilgore, Nacogdoches, Paris,
Tyler and Center and attracted some of the best golfers in
Texas including Jackie Cupit and his three brothers,
Homero Blancas (who once shot a 55 at one of these
tourneys), Billy Martindale, Don January, Charles Coody,
Dudley Wysong, Ben Crenshaw and the singing golfer Don
Cherry. It was usually a two-day event with qualifying on
Friday and the final round on Saturday. The Calcutta pool
was held on Friday night with players being auctioned off

Bar B Q, often with bands and dancing. Play began on Saturday and all the bets were settled that evening at another big party. It was a big deal in these towns and the locals turned out in droves to bet on their favorite player and party with the contestants. In 1982 the gambling got so big at Center (over $100,000) that the USGA and the NCAA cracked down on Calcutta pools effectively ending the tour.

In the summer of 1968 several us golf casual types headed east to Tyler to play at the Briarwood Invitational in one of the bigger tournaments on the Bar B Q tour. We had our photos taken that appeared in the newspaper and met some of the friendly locals. I remember the eventual winner there was Arnold Salinas who defeated a local teenage favorite in a thrilling sudden death playoff. Salinas was a good friend of both Trevino and Dick Martin and all three played at Tenison. Dick Martin was an excellent golfer and a local legend who won a lot of tournaments on the amateur circuit and separated many golfers from their money. He bet that day on Salinas.

Colwick tells the story that one day Frank Malone asked him if he wanted to play a best ball round at Tenison with two Hispanics who turned out to be Arnold Salinas and Lee Trevino. Fortunately for John and Frank the match never happened.

My friend Houston "Boscar" Satterwhite invited me to play in a one-day best ball tourney in his hometown of Breckenridge, which is about 130 miles due west of Dallas. It was in August 1963, and it was hot, dry and windy and the course was flat, hard, and fast. We shot a 67 that day and finished just out of the money. After the round we headed to the Club 180 for some beer. I had just sat down with a tall cold mug when several cowboys from the TLCB (Texas Liquor Control Board) sauntered over and asked me for my ID. Whoops! I was just one week shy of turning 21 – the legal age. Houston complained mightily, but that didn't matter one whoop to them, so it was off to jail where I paid my $50 fine and was released. Aside from that, the experience was fun.

I met Don Cherry, the singing golfer, in the most unlikely of places. It was on a cold New Years Eve night in 1968 and I was on my way back to Dallas from Oklahoma City. I had broken up with my girlfriend and was not feeling so good when checking into a hotel. There was a party in the next room and this guy saw me and said "come on in and join us, we are celebrating." He was Don Cherry and the party was fun!

A golf course is normally a safe sanctuary where one can enjoy the sport in relative freedom. Often it takes an act of God to get a man off the course or even a death in the immediate family…sometimes. The story goes like this…"a foursome was on the 16th green when an ambulance screamed past. One of the players said. "Excuse me gentlemen, may we have a moment of silence before putting out…there goes my wife to the hospital."

The Nelson

Whenever the Dallas Open (later the Byron Nelson) came to town I was there. The first Dallas Open was played at Lakewood Country Club in 1944 where Byron Nelson won easily. The following year Nelson won 11 consecutive tournaments, a record that will likely never be broken. I remember when the tournament was played at the old Preston Hollow Club in 1956, which later became the headquarters for EDS. Don January won the tourney on the 18th hole when he holed a sand shot. The next year the Dallas Open was played at Glen Lakes Country Club and was won by Sam Snead. I saw Snead play a memorable round at the Dallas Open in 1957 at Glen Lakes Country Club. He started the day by holing out a wedge shot on the first hole for an eagle and went on to shoot a 60! The Dallas Open moved to Oak Cliff Country Club the next year where it was played until 1968. I remember the home pro there, Earl Stewart, winning it in1961 – the only pro to ever have won a tournament on his home course.

In 1968 the tournament moved to Preston Trail and the name was changed to The Byron Nelson. For several years I posted scores of the leaders atop the leader board by the 18th green. Those at the top of the board who were under par got red numbers. As the last groups approached the green, I enjoyed teasing the gallery by waving a red number before posting it. Roger Meier Cadillac was a big sponsor of the Nelson and at times I picked up golfers in one of their Cadillac demos and took them to the course before their tee time. One day a golfer I had picked up earlier had a bad round, missed the cut and stormed off the course. He asked me to take him to the nearest liquor store and then to his hotel room. The Pavilion tent was the outdoor oasis for fun, food, booze and other debauchery. Floyd Dakil and his band often played there after dark and it was where the action took place after the last group finished. The Byron Nelson moved to Las Colinas Sports Club in Irving in 1982. The tournament, sponsored by the Salesmanship Club, is the largest and most successful charity event on the PGA tour raising millions for disadvantage kids.

Some of my favorite pros whom I followed at The Nelson:

Doug Sanders
Maurice Hudson, our Northwood pro, introduced me to Doug Sanders on the putting green before his round at Oak Cliff Country Club. They knew each other from their days in Georgia. Sanders was by far the most colorfully attired golfer on the tour whose wardrobe included purple, green, pink, yellow, and turquoise golf shoes, pants, and shirts. Dapper Doug was a great player as well with a very quick

and short back swing. He was good looking and always had quite a female following in the galleries. I remember him strutting down the fairway with the ubiquitous cigarette on one ear and a golf tee on the other. When I was a college student at Baylor, my friend Sam McCracken and I followed the pros from tournament to tournament. One weekend, we drove to Oklahoma City to see the OKC Open. We were following Sanders there when a huge thunderstorm with hail and lightning came up suddenly scattering galleries and golfers. We noticed some young lithesome lady with an umbrella run out onto the fairway to help cover Sanders and off they went.

Arnold Palmer was my favorite pro during the 60s. He burst upon the scene at Cherry Hills in Denver in the 1960 U.S. Open charging from 7 shots behind shooting a 65 the final day to win the championship. He began the round by firing 6 birdies on the first 7 holes! He overtook Mike Souchak, Julius Borus, Ben Hogan, and a young amateur Jack Nicklaus.   Palmer was responsible for enhancing and expanding the popularity of golf across the country.   I first saw him in person at Glen Lakes in the 19th hole and frequently followed him at the Byron Nelson.

Lee Trevino, aka the "Merry Mex", was well known for years around Dallas as one of the areas best golfers. Coming from humble beginnings, Trevino did not enjoy the advantages of being a country club golfer and was self-taught. He was born in 1939 and lived in a small shack near Glen Lakes Country Club. He often hit balls, sometimes with a Dr Pepper bottle, at Hardy's – a driving range with a crude 9-hole pitch and putt course on Lovers Lane and Greenville Avenue and owned by Hardy Greenwood. After his service in the Marine Corps, Trevino returned to Dallas and often played and gambled at Tension. The fairways and greens were hard and fast at Tenison, and later, when Trevino was winning on the PGA tour, he often credited his great short game to those days playing at Tenison. "When you have to hole a 6 foot putt to avoid paying someone $20 with only a dollar in your pocket… that is real pressure."

In the mid 1960s Titanic Thompson, a local golfer and well-known hustler, arranged a two-day money match between Trevino and Raymond Floyd. Floyd was a rising star on the PGA tour and Trevino had moved to El Paso to take a job at Horizon Hills Country Club. When Floyd arrived he came up to Trevino and asked him whom he was suppose to play – Lee said, "It's me!" The first day Floyd shot a 65 and lost by 3 shots. The next day he shot a 66 and lost by 2 shots. Thompson was down several thousand dollars and was ready to leave but Floyd begged to play one more day, doubling down on the money he lost. At the 18th, a par 5, the match was dead even. Floyd holed his eagle putt and Trevino's lipped out. After this experience, Floyd said, "be sure to know your opponent."

Trevino was quite the jokester and once pulled a rubber snake out of his bag on the first tee of a playoff with Nicklaus. Nicklaus lost that day and has said that Trevino was one of the best shot makers he has ever seen.

Trevino was struck my lightning when playing in the 1975 Western Open near Chicago. It affected his back and he was plagued by spasms after the incident. Later, as the myth goes, during a thunderstorm, Trevino was seen carrying an iron walking down the fairway. When told to run for cover, it is said that Trevino said, no worries, even God can't hit a one iron!

Tiger Woods was an outstanding amateur golfer who was taught the game at age two by his father. I first saw him at an NCAA collegiate tournament in Albuquerque when he was playing for Stanford. I was there for a Big Red 4 ball tournament and watched him pound dozens of balls 300 yards into the distance with his driver. I watched him play the last holes that day and his concentration was amazing. Stanford won and Woods shot the lowest score. We got his autograph that day for our 4-year-old son John. After turning pro in 1996 Woods set the PGA tour on fire and has won 79 events as of this writing trailing only Sam Snead (82) for most victories. He won the 2000 U. S. Open by 15 shots, has 3 Masters championships and holds 14 major golf titles. His spectacular record speaks for itself and he must be considered to be one of the best golfers of all time.

The Tiger joke goes like this: Playing in heaven, a few groups had gathered at the first tee, a 200 yard par 3 over a lake watching a golfer try to hit a 9 iron over the lake only to see ball after ball splash into the water. One of the guys asked the fellow's caddy, "Who does he think he is...Jesus Christ? Caddy responds, "He is Jesus but he thinks he is Tiger Woods."

Jack Nicklaus

The Golden Bear had a sterling amateur career at Ohio State. In 1959 at the age of 20, he won the United States Amateur at the Broadmoor defeating the great amateur from Oklahoma Charlie Coe who had won it the previous year. The following year he was runner up to Arnold Palmer at the US Open. Dudley Wysong, whose family  belonged to Northwood, made it to the finals of the US Amateur in 1961 in Pebble Beach to face Jack Nicklaus. Nicklaus won 8-6 in the 36 hole final match play round.

The first time I saw Nicklaus was at the 1963 PGA that was played at the Dallas Athletic Club. Those four days were scorchers with temperatures well over 100 degrees. I was getting a coke at a drink stand between holes when Nicklaus came over, said hello, and ordered a giant coke in the biggest cup they had. Nicklaus won the tournament which was his 3rd major and he was just 22! He went on to win a record 18 majors, finishing with his historic victory at the 1986 Masters when he was 46.

The Brook Hollow Golf Club

Brook Hollow was one of my favorite courses.   It was always in immaculate condition and its bent grass greens were the best in the metroplex. In fact, the club was the second in the area to get bent grass greens with Colonial in Ft. Worth being the first.

When I heard there was going to be qualifying at Brook Hollow for the US Amateur in1961, I called the local USGA Amateur Director, O'Hara Watts, for an application.

Watts, a longtime member of Brook Hollow, was one of the best amateurs in Texas and won the 1940 Texas PGA championship. The US Amateur qualifying was to be a 36-hole one-day medal play at Brook Hollow with the lowest scores qualifying to move forward. I was paired with this really good amateur from Midland. On the front nine I was terribly inaccurate from the tees and the fairways but was able to get up and down and sink a lot of putts that kept my score hovering near par. I finished the first 18 holes about 4 or 5 over but then the wheels came off on the 9th hole of the second 18 holes. On the 9th hole I duck hooked my tee shot high over the trees onto the pool patio scattering sunbathers where it bounced into the bushes landing below the dining room window. Took a triple bogey and was done!

Jack and Jane Munger took me to Brook Hollow several times to play and I remember the pro there was Larry Nabholz. Nabholz had trained the squirrels to come into the golf shop and eat acorns from his hand. One of the great amateur golfers there over many years was Herb Durham who won the club championship many times and regularly shoots his age today. Jack's brother in law Edwin Hopkins was a member and a great amateur golfer in Texas. I saw him play in the Texas Amateur – he possessed a great long fluid swing and could hit the ball a country mile.

Brook Hollow was considered one of the most exclusive of the country clubs in Dallas. (It should be noted that all the clubs considered themselves to be "exclusive"). The membership rolls there, like DCC, Lakewood and later Northwood, read like a who's who of Dallas civic, social and business society. Memberships were comprised of early Dallas pioneers and business entrepreneurs whose sons and daughters would continue this spirit of growth in the burgeoning city. Major deals were made on the course or in the 19th hole. Debutante parties, wedding receptions, charitable and philanthropic events, and the like were held there all year around.

Brook Hollow was founded in the early months of 1920 by Dallas Country Club golfers – Cam Buxton, Charles Dexter and H.L. Edwards. Buxton was a good amateur golfer and a golf course designer in Philadelphia before arriving in Dallas in 1916. His sister Caro lived in Dallas and was married to Edwards.

Edwards was born in Wales in 1856 and moved to America around 1880. Next he moved to Texas to become a rancher and cotton broker in Greenville. In 1890 he moved his company HL Edwards and Co. to Dallas. In 1896 he and his friend Richard Potter rented land at the corner of Oak Lawn and Lemmon Ave. and built an 18-hole golf course there, which was chartered as the Dallas Golf and Country Club later to be known as the Dallas Country Club. Edwards was the first President of the Texas Golf Association and was known as the "father of Texas golf".

Charles Dexter was an early member of the Dallas Country Club and good friend of Edwards. Dexter was lanky, tall and one of the great early golfers in Dallas. He won several amateur championships including the Southern Amateur and the Texas Amateur.

Buxton, Edwards and Dexter searched and found a place out west that was far from the Dallas Country Club and downtown Dallas. Back then the City of Dallas had about 160,000 citizens. In 1920, a dozen men met with Buxton, Dexter and Edwards to organize the new club. A charter from the State of Texas was issued in March, and a golf course architect, A.W. Tillinghast was hired. By the end of the year Brook Hollow had over 100 members.

The course was laid out over some gentle rolling farmlands that had belonged to several families. The Elm Fork of the Trinity River ran through it. There were plenty of beautiful towering oak, elm and cottonwood shade trees. It was perfect terrain for a golf course. Tillinghast was known as one of the best golf course architects of the times and had previously designed nearly 70 courses including Balustrol, Winged Foot, Brackenridge in San Antonio, and Cedar Crest in Dallas. Brook Hollow took nearly 4 years to complete. He also redesigned the Lakewood Country Club's course.

The members began playing when the front nine opened in 1921 but the full 18 was not ready for another three years. The Texas Amateur was played there in 1924. Also, in November of 1924, the great Bobby Jones played an exhibition match at Brook Hollow. Jones had just won the U. S Amateur in September and he agreed to play a charity match with Cam Buxton, Charles Dexter and Louis Jacoby. Fred Schoellkoph Jr. caddied for Jones. Jones shot a 73 and with his partner Buxton won the match. Walter Haig, the crown prince of golf, played there and reportedly won a lot of money from the locals. Brook Hollow was built as a golf club and not until later would it become a country club.

The old clubhouse was actually an old airport hangar. During the 30s badminton tournaments were popular and the players were required to wear all white. A swimming pool was also added. Charles Dexter was the best golfer winning the club championship several times. In 1934 the club hosted the Trans-Mississippi with Harry Todd and Spec Goldman tying for medalist honors. Slot machines were brought in and the club was sued for liquor violations. Seven clay tennis courts were built and Roy Bettis and Al Hill Sr. were perhaps the best tennis players then.

The old timers still talk about one of the greatest matches of all times that took place in 1936 between a young Jack Munger and the "veteran" Charles Dexter who held the course record of 64. It was the semi-finals of the club championship and Munger shot a 31 on the front nine. Dexter shot a 30 on the back nine to Munger's 34 which left both men tied at 65 after 18 holes. In sudden death both halved the first hole. On the second hole Dexter ended the epic match with a birdie.

The 40's saw the club expand in membership and stature. Joe Thompson, the founder and CEO of the 7-11 convenience stores, was elected president. Big bands, orchestras, dances, clambakes, and bingo games were common. Joseph Dey, the Executor Director of the USGA, joined the club in 1944. His local ties to members in Dallas would prove very helpful when Northwood later applied to host the 1952 US Open. In 1946, Brook Hollow hosted the Texas Amateur Championship in May and in September the club hosted the Dallas Open. The Salesmanship Club hosted a benefit for a children's camp the night before the tournament. Total prize money was

$10,000. Some of the big name gofers were there: Hogan, Snead, Lloyd Mangrum, and Jimmy Demaret. Ben Hogan won with a 72 hole score of 284 collecting $2,000.

The old clubhouse airplane hangar burned down in November 1948. Unfortunately, a huge cocktail party was scheduled for the next afternoon to be hosted by Mr. and Mrs. Estill Heyser, Jr. The party went ahead anyway, despite the smoldering ruins, with waiters in fire hats and slickers. Howard K. Smith designed the new clubhouse that would contain some 24,000 square feet. During the construction Neiman Marcus brought in the rich paneling, Leo Corrigan donated chandeliers, "Billie" Sedwick designed the interior, and Joe Lambert designed the landscape. The new clubhouse opened on July 25, 1949.

Brook Hollow was the home course of many of Texas greatest amateur golfers. During the 50s Herb Durham emerged as one of the best who continually won championships for several decades. Durham was the medalist at the Southern Amateur in 1951, won the Trans Mississippi in 1961 and the Brook Hollow Club Championship 11 times. Other notable golfers there were Jack Munger, Ed Hopkins, O'Hara Watts, Bill McBee, Jr., Joe Bob White, Wilson Schoellkoph, Jr., Don Addington and more recently Chip Stewart, Billy McBee, Jr.. and David Leachman.

The Dallas Country Club

The first country club in Texas had its beginnings in 1896 at some vacant lots that were in reality cow pastures. The property was bounded by Lemmon Avenue, Cedar Springs, Wellborn, Oak Lawn, Blackburn and Turtle Creek. The first golfers there were H.L. Edwards, 'the father of Dallas golf", and Richard E. Potter who strung some barbwire and rope together to keep out the cattle and then dug holes for tin cans. A nine-hole course of 2,137 yards was carved out and in 1897 the first un-chartered country club in Texas was formed. It would become The Dallas Country Club. J. T. Trezevant who had never played the game was among the first golfers at the new club. He was passing by the vacant lots in his buggy when he saw some men swinging clubs. It was not long before he became hooked on the game and would be instrumental in the development of the club. In 1898, the first golf tournament was played in Dallas and was won by J.C. O'Conner. The club was officially chartered on January 17, 1900. That year fifty-five acres were purchased, the first clubhouse was built and Mr. Trezevant was elected to be the first president. Another 9 holes were added to make it a short 18-hole golf course. The club hired their first golf pro, Mr. Bolton from Chicago. Richard (Old Dick) Fenby was chosen by the board to design and build the first clubhouse near Lemmon and Oak Lawn that cost approximately $2,000. The DCC held the first state tournament in 1903, which Edwards won. He died in 1947 at 91 and was inducted into the Texas golf Hall of fame.

In 1904 the members elected to build a new and bigger clubhouse. The second one was built near the first for a sum of about $25,000 on Oak Lawn. But on January 30, 1908, a fire burned down the clubhouse. Trezevant announced that the club would rebuild right away and the third clubhouse was built near the same spot that same year for $40,000. Meanwhile, Sam Leake, H.L Edwards and Robert Ralston searched for property to the north.

The 1912 DCC clubhouse and golfers on the first tee.
Photo by Frank Rogers and Son.

The Town of Highland Park wanted the club to move there to be the centerpiece of their new residential development. Hugh Prather and Edgar Flippen spearheaded this effort offering the club 50 acres at their cost to move to the new town. Later they increased the offer to 115 acres for $30,000. The Golf Realty Company was formed. John Armstrong's widow Alice deeded 56 acres in Highland Park to the company. In 1909 the members who wished to join were required to pay $150 for a share of stock in the Golf Realty Company and would then pay $3 per month dues to the club. $75,000 in 10 year bonds were issued at 6% interest, which were sold to build the new golf course and clubhouse. The new corporation was named The Dallas Country Club and it filed its charter on March 30, 1911. Initial memberships were limited to 500. The new clubhouse was estimated to cost between $40,000 to $50.000. A dam was erected on Turtle Creek that created a large swimming pool for the members. The "swimming hole" was a popular spot for families during the hot summers. The lake would become known as Lake Exall.

Thomas Bendelow had designed scores of golf courses and was chosen to design the new course for the Dallas Country Club. He would later design Lakewood CC. The new 18-hole course design would be over 6,000 yards and it was completed in 1912. The new club opened with a tournament on George Washington's birthday February 22, 1912. Sam A. Leake with George Aldridge won the President's Cup with H.L Edwards a close second. A big gala event marked the grand opening with an afternoon tea and an evening dinner with an orchestra. The Dallas Country Club immediately became the social scene of Dallas society. It was featured in the Dallas Society Magazine with photos of the grand ballroom and the exterior.

For nearly 50 years the 4th clubhouse would serve its members well but age had taken its toll. For several years there was much discussion and bickering over whether to build a new one with a new design or remodel the existing one. Finally, in 1955, it was decided that a new clubhouse would be built. The architectural firm of Harper and Kemp was selected to design it. In 1957 the 5th clubhouse opened.

Perhaps the best golfers during the roaring twenties were George Rotan and Charles Dexter. Rotan won or was runner up at the Texas Golf Association Championship for 4 straight years. L. R Munger, George Aldridge and Louis Jacoby were excellent golfers as well. In May 1921 the DCC hosted the Texas Golf Association amateur open, which was won by Charles Dexter who also won it the following year. He won the 1st annual DCC Invitational in October 1925.

During the roaring twenties the club hosted many gala parties. Although prohibition was in effect for a while, the members seemed to find ways around it. Saturday night dances were very popular and became weekly events well into the 30s and 40s. Big band orchestras played well into the night and dinner was often served outdoors. Debutante, sorority and fraternity parties were often held at the club and it was the focal point of the social scene in Dallas.

The Dallas Country Club was the home course of some of the best young amateur golfers in the country. Bud McKinney, Gus Moreland, O'Hara Watts, and David "Spec" Goldman were offered free junior memberships to play competitive matches against other club teams. Bud McKinney won the low qualifier in the 1931 USGA amateur with a 36 hole score of 140. Moreland won the Texas State Amateur in 1931, tied for 2nd in the 1932 US Amateur, finished 7th in the US Open in 1933 and won all 4 matches in the Walker Cup against England. He would win the state tournament 2 more times. O'Hara Watts won the DCC championship in 1934 as well as many other amateur tournaments.   Spec Goldman won it in 1936. Bud McKinney won the DCC championship in 1951 and 1961 and the Senior Championship 5 times.   Jack Munger won it in 1939 and 1940. Don Addington won championships at both Brook Hollow and DCC.

The Western Amateur was played at the DCC in April of 1950 that brought a great amateur field to Dallas including Charlie Coe, Don Addington, Gus Moreland,

Jack Munger, Spec Goldman, Bob Goldwater, Jimmy Vickers, Don Cherry, Frank Stranahan and others. Ben Hogan served as honorary tournament chairman. Charlie Coe, who won the national amateur and the Trans-Miss a year earlier, defeated Addington in the quarter-finals and won the tournament beating Bob Goldwater, the brother of Senator Barry Goldwater, in the finals 7-6.

Addngton, like fine wine, seems to get better with age. Recently, at the age of 80 he won the super seniors tournament at The Champions in Houston shooting a 4 under par 67! He was inducted into the Texas Golf Hall of Fame in 2011.

Don Addington

Bud McKinney was the lowest qualifier in the country for the 1931 U S Open. Forty years later he shot a 69 winning the Texas State Seniors for the third time! McKinney won many amateur and senior championships over his golfing career. He played golf over 7 decades into the 90's and it is estimated that he shot his age over 300 times. Dr. Brandon Carrell whose father Dr. William B. Carrell founded Carrell

Clinic and Scottish Rite Hospital, was an avid golfer at the club for over five decades until his death in 1981. He amassed many championship and runner- up trophies and was seen virtually daily on the course. Dr. Carrell was well respected in the medical community for his research on polio. When I came down with a various form of polio at age 16, my parents called Dr. Carrell who immediately came over to our house and diagnosed it. His quick diagnosis led to immediate treatment and to a full recovery. Recent champions at Dallas Country Club are Sam Manning, Steve Summers and Tim Gamso.

DCC hosted the first Texas Women's Golf Association tournament in May 1920 with over 50 golfers competing. The first women's club championship at DCC was held in 1924, and was won by Mrs. Herbert Jester. For the next few decades several ladies emerged as the best golfers winning multiple championships. Mary Nell Weatherred won the championship 10 times, Jane Munger won it 5 times and Nancy Swenson, in addition to her many tennis championships, won it 5 times. Mary Neil and Jane also served as presidents for the TWGA.

Bill McKenzie was the golf pro at the DCC for many years until he retired in 1953. Bobby Morris, the assistant pro, took his place and served until 1964 when Ross Collins followed him. Eldridge Miles was the assistant pro under Collins at the DCC and had played on the PGA tour for a while. He became the pro at Dallas Country Club in 1968 until 1974 before taking the head pro position at Bent Tree Country Club. Clayton Cole succeeded Miles in 1974 and remained the head pro there until 1986. Following Cole was Billy Harris who is the current pro.

Some fifty years after the 5th clubhouse was built, a growing consensus emerged for a new and bigger one. After much discussion and planning the membership voted overwhelmingly to approve plans to begin construction of a brand new clubhouse. It would be built closer to Turtle Creek, contain over 100,000 square feet and its exterior design would be Old English. The total cost was estimated to be over 50 million dollars. The interiors would have tall soaring wood beamed ceilings, mahogany walls, large glass windows to view the creek and golf course, ballrooms, several dining areas and multiple fireplaces.   For the grand opening night the members literally received the red carpet treatment and were treated to much fanfare including several bands, large extravagant buffets, "movie stars" and an amazing ice sculpture. It opened in February 2012.

Sandy and Susie McDonough at the grand opening

View of the new DCC clubhouse from the pools

Epilogue

During his later years Dad's eye disease, macular degeneration, worsened and he was unable to play golf. He asked me to type a letter of resignation to Northwood. Since golf was such a big part of his life, it was with a great deal of sadness that I did. For many years he would fondly recall the many moments and memorable rounds that he shared with me. He remembered his hole in ones, the rounds he shot, the courses he played and the friends he made.

Perhaps the most poignant memory came when Dad was at home in hospice care. One afternoon I entered his room and saw him sitting up in bed clasping his hands and wagging them back and forth. I asked, "what are you doing Dad"? He said, "playing golf of course."

Dad passed peacefully on February 17, 2001, at the age of 88. No doubt he has joined his pals and is playing golf daily on heavenly courses.

Samuel "Sandy" McDonough is a life long resident of Dallas who loves the game of golf. Although he rarely plays these days due to other life's commitments such as marriage, kids, job and other circumstances, his remembrances of golf remain vivid.

Sandy is a graduate of Highland Park High School and Baylor University and lives in Dallas with his wife Susie. He has three sons: Robert, Joe, and John. A successful businessman, he is a Realtor with Virginia Cook Realtors. Previous books that he has authored are:

Our Founding Fathers Homes and Churches in Virginia

A Sailor Returns Home

The Faith that Saved a Nation

He can be contacted by email:
sandymcd@sbcglobal.net

Bibliography

Sampson, Curt. "A Dallas Classic" Lakewood Country Club 1912-2012

Glenn, Rhonda. "Brook Hollow Golf Club" 1920-1995. Taylor Publishing Company 1995

Galloway, Diane Caylor. "Dallas Country Club" The first 100 Years. Book Production: Gifford Touchtone and Ed Doran. Dallas Country Club 1996.

Stricklin, Art. "A History of Northwood Club" 1946 – 2002. Thanks for the Memories. The Downing Company Publishers 2002.

Wheeler, Pat. "Tales From the Late Great Beer and BBQ Circuit" Austin Brothers Publishing. Keller, Texas

Munger, Marilyn. Personal collection of photographs and recollections.

Special Thanks to members past and present of Northwood, Brook Hollow Golf Club, Lakewood Country Club and Dallas Country Club.

Much of the events and materials in the book can be attributed to web sites, links, and searches found on Google and Yahoo. So I am grateful to these Internet sources and of course to Al Gore for inventing the Internet.

Editing thanks to Mardi and Allen Myers, Milton Gish, Tommy Newsome, Gene Wilson and Susie McDonough.

Thanks also to my friends at St. Michaels and All Angels Church and at the Preston Group for their spiritual fellowship.